**Attention:**

I want you to take note that this book is intended to be used in conjunction with our *Parenting, Movement, & Nutrition* multimedia training material. Much of the subject matter in this book refers to topics discussed within these additional resources. You can find these components of the *Parenting, Movement, & Nutrition* project at our website:

www.saatkampcommunications.com.

Welcome to the *Parenting, Movement, & Nutrition* family!

Peace,
Dr. Mike Saatkamp

"There are many books available as a resource for parents to help their children. There are very few to support the parents and caregivers. This book and the accompanying video will bring skill and confidence to parents facing the challenge and *blessing* of a special needs child."

*-- Dr. Robert Melillo*
*Founder, Brain Balance Achievement Centers*

"I read this thoughtful and informative book with pleasure and when I finished it, I wanted more. I recommend this as a resource for any parent of a special needs child."

*-- Dr. David Rosenberg*
*Board Certified in Pediatric Medicine*
*Milwaukee, Wisconsin*

"This is a very practical book, full of great tips that will strengthen families and communities."

*-- Nichole Elmendorf, OTR*
*Owner, Progressive Beginnings, Rehabilitation Specialists for Children with Special Needs*

"I've known Dr. Mike for 5 years, and I know his commitment to making this material available to families. He is a dedicated doctor, father, and community member."

*-- Kim Burch*
*Special Needs Grandmother*

# Parenting, Movement, & Nutrition

## For Special Needs Families

### How Special Needs Parents Can Strengthen Their Families and Themselves

Dr. Mike Saatkamp
Chiropractor & Special Needs Dad

iUniverse, Inc.
Bloomington

**Parenting, Movement, & Nutrition**
**For Special Needs Families**

Copyright © 2013 by Saatkamp Communication

All rights reserved. No part of this book may be used or reproduced by any means, graphic, electronic, or mechanical, including photocopying, recording, taping or by any information storage retrieval system without the written permission of the publisher except in the case of brief quotations embodied in critical articles and reviews.

iUniverse books may be ordered through booksellers or by contacting:

iUniverse
1663 Liberty Drive
Bloomington, IN 47403
www.iuniverse.com
1-800-Authors (1-800-288-4677)

Because of the dynamic nature of the Internet, any web addresses or links contained in this book may have changed since publication and may no longer be valid. The views expressed in this work are solely those of the author and do not necessarily reflect the views of the publisher, and the publisher hereby disclaims any responsibility for them.

ISBN: 978-1-4759-8170-4 (sc)

Printed in the United States of America

iUniverse rev. date: 03/25/2013

*for Shelly, Helena, and Maren*
*my inspiration and life support system*

# Acknowledgments

I stand on the shoulders of the giants in my life.

I thank from the bottom of my heart:

My wife Michelle, my loving companion on life's journey- who works tirelessly to care for our children, to meet every need of theirs that she can, and who has given me the time and permitted the use of our resources to produce this book.

My daughters Helena and Maren, the joy and pride of my life, who tolerate my study and writing time, who support me with their love and delight me with their demands for recreation and play.

My mom, Pat, and my dad, Fred, who raised me to love learning, people, and the UCLA Bruins.

The late Rev. Dr. Truman Barrett, my mentor for over 30 years, who tended to my intellectual and spiritual development.

Marie Hetzel, who supported me with her friendship and editorial skill from the beginning of this book through it's completion.

Dr. Ted Carrick, father of Functional Neurology. The F.R. Carrick Institute has given me access to the finest Functional Neurology training available.

My many instructors at the Carrick Institute, in particular Dr. Mike Powell, Dr. Robert Melillo, Dr. Adam Klotzek, Dr. Datis Kharrazian, and Dr. Brandon Brock.

There are many others. I am grateful to each one.

# Table of Contents

## Section 1 – Parenting

| | | |
|---|---|---|
| 1 | Life Is Difficult | 7 |
| 2 | Encouragement, Learning, and Effort | 14 |
| 3 | Keeping a Journal to Encourage Yourself | 17 |
| 4 | Teaching and Encouraging Others | 21 |
| 5 | How to Talk About the Brain | 25 |
| 6 | Being Wise | 29 |

## Section 2 – Movement

| | | |
|---|---|---|
| 7 | Thinking About Movement | 35 |
| 8 | Born to Make Connections | 39 |
| 9 | From Reflex to Awareness | 43 |

## Section 3 – Nutrition

| | | |
|---|---|---|
| 10 | A Healthy Brain Needs Three Things | 49 |
| 11 | As Much Protein As You Can Afford | 52 |
| 12 | The Problem with Sugar | 55 |
| 13 | Chronic Inflammation and Your Child's Brain | 58 |
| 14 | Healthy Belly, Healthy Brain | 62 |
| 15 | Good Fats and Color Foods: Choosing an Anti-Inflammation Diet | 66 |
| 16 | Exercise is Nutritious | 70 |
| 17 | How to Make Each Breath More Nutritious | 74 |
| 18 | Eating Together is Good Medicine | 78 |

## Section 4 – Communication & Leadership

| | | |
|---|---|---|
| 19 | Know Your Limitations and Get the Help You Need | 85 |
| 20 | Your Friends Want to Help You | 88 |
| 21 | Your Child's School Wants Him or Her to Succeed | 91 |
| 22 | Communicating with Your Insurance Carrier | 94 |
| 23 | Communicating with Government Agencies | 98 |
| 24 | A Good Parent is a Good Leader | 101 |

# Introduction

*"Take the first step in faith. You don't have to see the whole staircase, just take the first step."*

-Dr. Martin Luther King

I began writing this book several years ago. As I researched, I sifted through hundreds of articles on nutrition, movement, special needs families, and many neurological conditions. I've taken great care to select the most important information to help families of special needs kids profoundly improve their lives.

There are some people for whom this book was NOT written. This book is NOT for you if:

- You feel resigned to a life of drudgery.
- You are opposed to improving your health with good nutrition.
- You enjoy reading about your health and well-being, but are not interested in taking action to make your health better.
- If you are not willing to ask for help when you need it.
- You want to bypass your child's health care team and do it all yourself.
- You are not willing to share what you learn with others, so they, too, can improve their lives.

This book WAS written for you if:

- You know you are in a difficult situation and are willing to take proactive steps to learn and improve your life and the lives of your family members.
- You understand that nutrition and exercise are important, but need some help putting the sciences of nutrition and exercise to work for you.
- If you are willing to take what you learn and teach others in your community.

*Parenting, Movement, and Nutrition for Special Needs Families* is intended to be read in conjunction with the *Parenting, Movement, and Nutrition Workbook*. The workbook can be downloaded from the video training that accompanies this book.

You will benefit most if you:

1. Read this book

2. Watch each video

3. Download and read through the *Parenting, Movement, and Nutrition Workbook* and complete the questions and action steps

4. Do each of your *Parenting, Movement, and Nutrition* movement lessons

After you've completed your book, workbook, video training, and movement lessons, you may want to attend a *Parenting, Movement, and Nutrition* workshop. I hope you can attend the workshop. There

you will meet other parents of special needs kids, learn about the amazing research in nutrition and movement science that is directly applicable to your life, and you'll develop many new skills for making your life more fun, more wise, and more meaningful. A schedule of *Parenting, Movement, and Nutrition* workshops can be found on our website-
www.saatkampcommunications.com.

# Section 1
# Parenting

# Chapter 1
# Life Is Difficult

*"In the middle of the journey of my life, I came to myself, in a dark wood, where the true way was wholly lost."*

-Dante

My daughter Maren was born prematurely on October 1, 1991. She weighed one pound, 14 ounces, and was so tiny that I could fit my wedding ring around her upper arm. When I held her I thought the blanket she was wrapped in felt more substantial than she did. As I looked into her eyes for the first time, I did the best I could to hold her with steady hands, and to trust the expertise of the physicians at Columbia Hospital in Milwaukee, Wisconsin. The whirring of computers and hospital equipment, voices of nurses and doctors, crying of babies, and smells of sanitation merged into my brain, and so much was happening that I didn't have time to think the experience through. Just time to pretend I had it together.

I was scared out of my mind.

I wondered…how would I care for a child with special needs? How would I pay for all the necessary equipment, medical care, physical therapy, and occupational therapy? Would our insurance provide coverage? Would I be able to keep my business? Would Maren be able to talk? Walk? Would my family be able to help? Would friends pull away? Would I earn enough money to care for her even after my wife Shelly and I were gone?

I pretended to the world and to myself that I was up for the job, but deep inside, some parts of me stopped breathing. Sound familiar?

Maren was transferred to St. Joseph's Hospital, also in Milwaukee, where there was a neonatal intensive care unit. She stayed there for the next two and a half months. I came to visit for many hours every day, reading to her, and holding her once the doctors agreed that she could tolerate being held. I had learned that based on the tests Maren had been given, she was very likely to have moderate to severe cerebral palsy, though the doctors couldn't predict much about her condition. Dr. Greg Melville, Maren's neonatologist, told me that she might have a very mild case of CP (cerebral palsy) with only tight heel cords, or be severely involved and unable even to speak. I was grateful for his compassion and honesty.

I remember holding Maren and walking around the incubator room wondering what lay ahead. I was young and resilient and sturdy, but nothing in my life before Maren's birth had prepared me for the challenges I was preparing myself to confront.

Though I was very attentive to Maren and my family over the next few years, I didn't take very good care of myself. I ate a lot of food that was unhealthy for me, and I gained a lot of weight. I hardly exercised at all. I buried myself in my work because that was the only place I felt I had control. That wasn't good for the parts of me that weren't breathing. I was living with terrible stress, and I wasn't mature enough to find the help I needed.

In 1994, when Maren was three years old, I started to feel a little lightness coming back into my body. I remember sitting at my desk and picking up a copy of one of my favorite books, *The Road Less Travelled*, by M. Scott Peck. I had read the book many years earlier, when I was too young to understand the wisdom Dr. Peck offered. With a few more years under my belt, I looked at the opening line of the book with fresh eyes. It read:

"Life is difficult."

When I read that line, which I had read many times before as a younger man, I could breathe a little better. I also felt my muscles relax, and my vision cleared up some. Most noticeable, my hearing became very acute, as though waking up from a muffled sleep.

That was about 20 years ago. I'm no longer a young man facing a life-changing event. I'm 54 years old as I write this, and I've been the father of a special needs child for over 20 years. I know the challenges you are facing, the insecurity you feel, the panic that sets in when you don't get enough sleep, or you eat poorly, or you don't get enough exercise. I know the shame you feel when you can't fix your child's life for her, or when you can't shield him from the hurtful taunts and misunderstandings of those in your community who don't see through your child's disability to the pleasant soul within. I know the economic stress that leaves you feeling alone, scared, and misunderstood. I also know there is little time for proper nutrition and exercise.

I've written this book and organized the *Parenting, Movement, and Nutrition* multimedia material to give you tools to help you build a happy and resilient life even in difficult circumstances. To do this, in addition to my Chiropractic training, I've completed over 1,000 post-doctoral training hours in clinical neurology, and many thousands of hours of additional study. This book will help you write and live the story of your own life with vitality, enthusiasm, attuned communication, and resilience. I've spent many years studying nutrition, movement, and interpersonal neurobiology to make my own life, my family's life, and your life, better.

So I'm making you a promise. If you read this book carefully, study it thoughtfully, study the *Parenting, Movement, and Nutrition* video training thoughtfully, do the movement lessons many times, and then teach the material you've learned to a few other people, your life and the life of your child with special needs will change for the good.

I guarantee it. You will:

- Be a better parent and leader, and know it.
- Have a better sense of the meaning of your life.
- Be an effective champion for your child throughout his or her school career.
- Communicate with confidence to your insurance company, ensuring coverage for necessary physical and occupational therapy.
- Know which foods are best for you and for

- your child, and how healthy food will increase energy, reduce pain, improve movement, clarify thinking, and reduce risk of diabetes, Alzheimer's disease, bowel problems, heart disease, and many other chronic health conditions.
- Increase your well being and resilience.
- Learn to use your most valuable inner strengths.
- Understand how movement is nourishment for your brain.
- Learn how to face challenging situations and keep your sense of self intact.
- Be part of a learning community that shares knowledge in order to better our kids' lives.

The book is divided into four sections:

1. Section one teaches helpful ways to communicate with your child, and how we can improve resilience and well-being in our families.

2. Section two teaches how to improve movement, and how movement and breathing nourish the brain.

3. Section three teaches how good nutrition improves brain health.

4. Section four integrates the earlier chapters and offers helpful tips for communicating with schools, insurers, the state, and other institutions that you utilize on your child's behalf.

We'll delve into each section in more detail during the downloadable training. The movement lessons and workbook contain further information so you may continue your progress at home. The end of each chapter contains questions and action steps designed to deepen your understanding of the *Parenting, Movement, and Nutrition* material.

Let's get started!

Here are your first questions. See you in the next chapter.

# Questions & Action Steps

1. Write a clear, concise description of your child's special needs. Describe in simple language what it's like for you to get through a day caring for your special needs child.

2. Write a paragraph describing your current parenting abilities. Are you a good listener? Do you speak clearly on behalf of your child? Do you understand yourself to be credible as a parent?

3. Write a paragraph assessing your knowledge of movement. Do you exercise daily? Do you understand how movement affects your brain? Do you know how movement drives the development of your child's brain? Will you make a commitment to learning more about movement and how to increase movement in your life and in your child's life?

4. Write a paragraph assessing your knowledge of nutrition. Do you know which sugars are most healthy for you? Do you know what a protein is and what proteins do? Do you know which fats are good for you, and why? Do you know how oxygen is used to make energy in your body?

Don't worry if you can't answer all of the questions above… you will learn!

# Chapter 2
# Encouragement, Learning, and Effort

*"Instruction does much, but encouragement everything."*

-Johann Wolfgang von Goethe

Your brain changes with each new experience. Every new word, movement, or skill creates more connections between brain cells (neurons). This is called "neuroplasticity."

These connections are further strengthened by repetition. Activities like practicing movement, listening to music, and reading poetry are important to you and your special needs child.

Here's why:

Dr. Carol Dweck, currently a Stanford University professor, studied a group of students at risk for dropping out of school. She divided the students into two groups. The first group was shown a video that demonstrated how intelligence could be increased through hard work. The second group was shown a video that told them how smart they were.

The results?

The first group, told that intelligence could be improved through hard work, had a significantly lower dropout rate than the group that was told they were smart. In other words, the group that was encouraged to work hard proceeded to do just that and their efforts did, in fact, improve their intelligence. They worked hard and got smarter.

You and I can too.

Encouragement and enthusiasm for learning are important skills, but hard work is required to gain and retain new knowledge. Every time you encourage yourself to put effort into learning, you are harnessing your brain's power to make new connections while improving your intelligence.

Learning is not possible without effort, but the effort is worthwhile. Real learning means real improvement.

# Questions & Action Steps

1. Who encourages you? To whom do you look to for support when you aspire to learn?

2. Do you typically put an effort into learning new things? Explain.

3. Have you noticed that the more you learn, the better you feel? Recall a time this was true, and write it down.

- What could I do to help myself and my child flourish a little more tomorrow?

There are more sample journaling questions on the *Parenting, Movement, and Nutrition* website. I strongly encourage you to practice daily journaling. There will be many times that you will be your own best counselor.

## Questions & Action Steps

1. If you were to begin journaling on a daily basis, where could you find the tools you need? Do you have paper at home? Pens? A notebook? How soon could you start?

2. What other questions would you like to ask yourself on a daily basis? List three.

3. If you could write yourself a letter you wouldn't read for 30 years, what would you say? (Maybe that's the first question to start you on the road to daily journaling!)

# Chapter 4
# Teaching and Encouraging Others

*"To touch the soul of another human being is to walk on holy ground."*

-Dr. Stephen R. Covey

One of the most important ways to help your child flourish is to teach others about your child's special needs. Whatever your child's special needs, it's your job to communicate them to the people with whom he or she comes in contact. Most people know very little about autism, ADD/ADHD, cerebral palsy, spina bifida, genetic challenges, developmental delays, sensory integration issues, and the many other challenges faced by special needs children. They would probably like to learn from you.

Here are a few ways to teach and encourage people such as: teachers, school administrators, insurance adjustors, physical therapists, occupational therapists, and others:

1. Make it clear from the onset you know it takes work to engage with special needs kids and you are grateful for their help. Professionals are often expected to have solutions for your child, which they may or may not have, and they will be appreciative that you know they will have to work hard while assisting your child. Family members will appreciate your

2. forethought and will be better able to help.

3. Let them know you are grateful for their help, that sometimes you'll be exhausted and forget to say thanks, but that you are aware of the high quality of attention your special needs child requires. And let them be grateful to you! They know how hard you work.

4. Write a note thanking those who have helped. Acknowledge a particular time that someone said just the right word to help you or your child feel understood.

5. If your insurance agent or claims adjustor has difficulty determining whether physical or occupational therapy is necessary, take time to explain the concepts you are learning in this course: neuroplasticity (how the brain changes/improves), how movement increases brain function, and how PTs and OTs help organize the brain to improve the life of your child. (NOTE: Don't give up on the insurance industry, even if you get a claims adjustor who is oblivious to your situation. The only way insurance adjustors will learn the importance of your child's care is through clear communication.)

6. Ask your child's teachers and therapists what you can do at home to help your child reach his or her goals. Be clear about the limits of your time so you don't over commit.

7. Any time you have a chance to speak in front of a group like a parents' group, teachers' group, church group, or local business group, do it! You don't

need to sound like a university professor, just speak as a parent about your child's needs. Your words have power and credibility when you represent the special needs community. You can be a calm, deliberate, and effective advocate for your child, and for all of our kids.

# Questions & Action Steps

1. Write a clear, concise description of your child's special needs. Describe in simple language what it's like for your child to get through a day.

2. Write a clear, concise description of your experience as a parent of a special needs child. In what ways do you need help? In what ways are you succeeding?

3. What do you need to learn more about in order to make your life simpler, happier, and more effective?

# Chapter 5
# How to Talk About the Brain

*"... the use of our intelligence quite properly gives us pleasure. In this respect the brain is like a muscle. When we think well, we feel good. Understanding is a kind of ecstasy."*

-Dr. Carl Sagan

Dr. Carl Sagan was one of the greatest scientists of our time. He developed the PBS television series, *Cosmos*, bringing the intrigue and excitement of science to the masses. He was also the first and most effective scientist to teach the public about brain function.

My first exposure to brain science was in Dr. Sagan's Pulitzer Prize-winning book, *The Dragons of Eden*. In this book, Dr. Sagan presented the "triune brain" model. This model is no longer accepted as fact by the scientific community, but talking about the brain in this way can be helpful when you are just beginning. In the triune brain model, the brain is divided into three basic anatomical sections:

1. The reptilian brain
2. The mammalian brain
3. The human brain

The **reptilian brain** (also known as the brain stem)

controls basic functions such as: breathing, heart rate, balance, swallowing, sleeping, excreting, reproducing, and eye movements. All living animals have this structure (or a similar one). Most animals do not, however, do much more than these basic functions. They don't bond deeply with each other; in fact, they aren't interested in other animals at all unless they perceive one as a threat, a meal, or a mate. I once had a pet horned toad named 'Horney'. I really liked him, but he didn't notice me or anything else around him that wasn't a worm.

Caring is where the **mammalian brain** comes in. The mammalian brain is an extension of the reptilian brain and is present in all mammals- humans, dogs, bears, elephants, etc. It allows these animals to connect with each other and to find pleasure in doing so. The mammalian brain is important to our "fight or flight" response (how we respond to serious stress). Some of your ability to discern to whom you want to be close and from whom you want to flee takes place in the mammalian brain. Many scientists who study the science of bonding and attachment will tell you that the number one survival strategy you have (if you're willing to admit you're a mammal), is attachment. More on that later.

The **human brain**, the cortex, is the outermost, and most complex, part of your brain. The human brain is the most complex organ in the known universe. It allows us to use language, manipulate objects with our hands, move with purpose, have a conscience, plan for the future, remember important events, and create clear goals.

Even though the triune brain model has some

limitations (which we will discuss later in the book and workshop), it's a very good tool for understanding how the brain functions. For our purposes, it will help you understand your child's special needs. (This will also help you explain your child's special needs to others. Most people want to be helpful and relate to your child. You can help them feel more competent and less fearful.)

This is why it's important to learn the basic anatomy of the triune brain model. It's our responsibility to educate our community about our special needs children.

# Questions & Action Steps

1. Write a short description of the reptilian brain. What are its functions?

2. Write a short description of the mammalian brain. How is our sense of bonding common to all mammals, not just humans?

3. Write a description of the human brain. What are the distinctions between the human brain and the brains of other mammals?

# Chapter 6
# Being Wise

*"What I'm after isn't flexible bodies, but flexible brains. What I'm after is to restore each person to human dignity."*

-Moshe Feldenkrais

Learning about brain function, physical movement, and nutrition gives you an added benefit- you'll learn to describe your life (and that of your child) in specific, scientific language. This new knowledge will reflect decades of research, empowering you to speak with credibility and conviction on behalf of your special needs child. Knowledge really is power.

In the world of science, documentation is important. Credible research is collected, organized, performed, reviewed, and widely distributed. Other scientists review all research. If the research study is accepted, it gets published. That's called "peer review". When a research paper is peer-reviewed and published, it can be cited for use in other research as established science.

That makes scientific literature very important for those of us with special needs children. You can trust that peer-reviewed literature is accurate within the limits of the method used for study.

Here's my caveat about scientific literature. While

science is a rational enterprise, facts evolve and change as new information becomes available. We make choices using the best information we can find and align the scientific facts with our lives as we understand them. In other words, science is our tool, but as any good scientist will tell you, science is *always* a work in progress.

That being said, I am certain your child will be happier, healthier, and more successful if you spend some time each day researching on his or her behalf.

You will find, if you haven't already, that as you consult with scientific journals, professionals, teachers, psychologists, insurers, and state agencies, it will be you who makes the big decisions on behalf of your special needs child. This book and training program will help you navigate this lifetime process.

# Questions & Action Steps

1. Write a few sentences describing how you make choices when you don't have enough information. Do you research on the Internet? Do you contact a friend? Do you study books, call schools, or watch educational television?

2. Comment on the quality of information you receive from health professionals, school professionals, and state agencies. How could you supply them with better information, even as you seek their help?

The next chapter begins your training in the science and art of movement, and how it applies specifically to you and your child.

# Section 1 References

Many of the topics I've written about in Section 1 can be further explored in:

1. *The Developing Mind*, Daniel J. Siegel M.D.

2. *Parenting From The Inside Out*, Daniel J. Siegel, M.D.

3. *Mind Set*, Carol Dweck, Ph.D.

*Section 2*

*Movement*

# Chapter 7
# Thinking About Movement

*"Children learn with their bodies before they learn with their minds."*

-Sally Goddard Blythe

By far, the best way to learn about movement is to move, and pay careful attention to the quality of your movement. In some ways, thinking and talking about movement distracts us from our direct perception. So we need to do the following to improve our understanding of movement:

- Practice your Parenting, Movement, and Nutrition Movement Lessons… a few introductory lessons are included in your video and audio training
- Study scientific literature about movement
- Study movement literature from experts in movement-related fields, such as physical therapists, occupational therapists, chiropractors, and yoga instructors
- Learn to carefully observe movement

Through these practices we can explore the following questions:

1. How do you learn to move?

2. How does your brain modify a movement while

you are moving?

3. How do you distinguish between good movement and poor movement?

4. How do you improve movement, and what does that mean?

5. What constitutes improved movement?

6. How does movement link directly to language development?

7. How is movement supported by good nutrition? Or damaged by poor nutrition?

8. How can you communicate your knowledge about movement to others?

You will best learn about movement from the inside out, by actually moving your own body. Your own movement experience is your best teacher. Slow down and learn from your breathing, posture, and muscle tension. The more you understand about your own movement, the better you will appreciate the way your child moves. You'll also learn to appreciate how movement is linked to behavior (yours and your child's).

As your movement improves, so will your ability to think. You will make deeper distinctions between fast and slow movements, how you move toward or away from certain people and situations, and how you feel around others. This will give you insight into how your child feels around others so you can better support him or her in difficult situations.

As you talk about your *Parenting, Movement, and Nutrition* movement lessons, you will find that you are better equipped to describe movement to others. You will help them to understand your child's abilities and/or limitations, which will open a new world to your child and to those with whom he or she communicates.

Learning about movement will be one of the most rewarding experiences of your life. From the outside, it may not appear exciting, but that's because it's an inside job- one of the most intimate observations about yourself that you can make. As you improve this skill, you will see that movement is like a nutrient. This "nutrient" is necessary for brain health. Understanding this is crucial for you and your special needs child.

# Questions & Action Steps

1. Comment on whether or not you knew there was a link between movement and language development before reading this chapter and the training material. How does that information change your view of the importance of movement?

2. Write a few paragraphs describing your own movement experiences. Are you graceful? Clumsy? Is your balance good? How do you assess that?

3. Comment on the movement of your special needs child. Is he or she stiff? Awkward? Strong? How do you feel as you make these comments? How could you describe your child's movement in a positive, helpful way?

4. After you've listened to the movement lessons, comment on your contact with the floor before and after your lesson. Were your muscles relaxed? Or tense? Did you have a clear sense of your skeleton?

5. Think of people you have known with physical limitations from conditions such as strokes, cerebral palsy, or Parkinson's disease. How did their movement difficulties affect their life?

# Chapter 8
# Born to Make Connections

*"The self-organization of the developing brain occurs in the context of a relationship with another self, another brain."*

-Allan Schorre

At birth, your brain was an incompletely connected mass of cells called "neurons". Prior to that, the driving force behind your development was genetic. While genes are important to brain development throughout your lifetime, there is another factor that empowers us to nurture and enhance our genetic inheritance: epigenetics.

The science of epigenetics studies the environment's effect on your genes, specifically, what causes your genes to make certain proteins. Many factors act on your genes. Stress, hunger, exercise, music, learning, blood sugar level, oxygen intake, and environmental input will effect your body and cause changes in gene expression. In particular, movement and nutrition are important epigenetic factors.

Genes (your cells' protein-making machinery) are acted upon by your environment from the moment you are conceived. Since you can't change your genes, you can focus on epigenetics-- altering your nutrition, movement, and stress. In other words, learning to improve your health.

Babies are born with billions of nerve cells that are destined, over his or her lifetime, to make trillions of connections. Building those connections takes a long time. When you observe a newborn, you won't notice much movement. Newborns can't hold up their head, sit, crawl, walk, or speak.

What *can* a newborn do? He or she can react to loud noises with a startle reflex, pull away from pain with a withdrawal reflex, and find his or her mother's nipple with a rooting reflex. He or she can digest, but not that well. Vision is developing, but there is no understanding of what's being seen. Newborns are completely dependent on their caretakers.

This is an interesting situation. Human beings have the longest childhood developmental period of any other creature. When a foal is born, for example, it wobbles on spindly legs for only half an hour before it's off and running around the ranch. Humans, on the other hand, take a year just to stand steadily and begin to walk.

Why? A horse is born with most of the abilities required for survival. But a human baby has to learn motor control, language, complex problem solving, and skills like reading, singing, building, and listening.

At the root of these developmental skills is movement. Every time your child learns to move in a new way, his or her genes create new proteins. These proteins build a more complex brain by making additional connections, called "synapses", between nerve cells. That's why movement is profoundly important to your child's healthy brain development.

As further movement is learned, more synapses are formed, and your child develops from a helpless little being into one who can lift his or her head, look around, sit up, crawl, stand, vocalize, speak, and learn to communicate with others.

None of these skills will develop in the absence of movement. This is especially important for those of us with children who have movement disorders like cerebral palsy. Our kids need extra help to develop to their fullest potential.

The *Parenting, Movement, and Nutrition* movement lessons content was designed with special attention to learning about movement from the inside out, so that you can understand how to better assist your child. I encourage you to perform the lessons many times (repetition is the best teacher). You can use your knowledge of movement to make a better brain for yourself.

# Questions & Action Steps

1. Recall how your child learned to move. Did he or she learn easily? Were there periods of struggle?

2. Comment on the special needs children in your community. What do you notice about their ability to move?

3. When you observe the movement challenges that many children and adults face, do you think local restaurants and public places are doing enough to accommodate their needs? What action could you take to improve the lives of special needs people in your community?

4. Comment on your own movement history. Did you enjoy dancing? Athletics? Did you have good balance? Comment on how your movement matured since you were a child.

# Chapter 9
# From Reflex to Awareness

*"A well trained nervous system is the greatest friend a mind can have."*

-Halleck

During your child's development, he or she will learn to move. Her motor skills will evolve from primitive reflexes to intentional movements. Primitive reflexes are organized by the brain stem, also known as the reptilian brain. Here are some examples:

**The Moro Reflex-** the Moro Reflex is present in utero. It appears about 12 weeks after conception and continues to develop throughout pregnancy. When an infant is exposed to a sudden change in head position, like when the head is dipped backward as he or she is picked up or set down, the baby's arms and legs will fling out as he or she takes a deep breath and cries. As this reflex matures, at about four months, he or she will instead consciously raise his or her shoulders and look around when startled. This is one of the first stages in the development of attention. The Moro Reflex can also be triggered by sudden flashes of light, loud sounds, quick changes in temperature, and smoke. If the Moro reflex isn't overcome, or "integrated", it may result in:

- Balance problems
- Poor coordination
- Sensory integration challenges

- Difficulty with eye movements
- General anxiety

**The Tonic Labyrinthine Reflex-** the Tonic Labyrinthine Reflex (TLR) is a response to the forward or backward movement of the head. When you support and lower the baby's head below the body, her arms and legs will extend. If you support and lift her head, her arms and legs will flex. This is how she will learn to control the position of her head in relation to her body-- an important step in learning to look up, sit, and stand. The TLR is one of the important ways an infant learns to cope with gravity. If the TLR is poorly integrated, it may result in:

- Balance problems
- Posture problems
- Vertigo/dizziness
- Walking on toes
- Difficulty integrating vision and sound

Mature motor skills emerge from these early reflex patterns. Once you know what to look for, observing your child's movement becomes fascinating. You'll see him or her evolve from using reflexive movements to movements of consciousness and intent as the brain becomes better connected. You are witnessing the emergence of a human being who can make choices and interact with others, one who can notice how he or she feels, and begin to sense what life is like for other people. This is the beginning of compassion.

# Questions & Action Steps

1. Do you take time each day to relax your breathing and pay attention to movement? How could you find a few extra minutes in your daily schedule to practice deep breathing and muscle relaxation?

2. Comment on how the primitive reflexes become intentional movements. Does this surprise you? Write a sentence or two on how this might change the way you see the importance of movement.

3. Describe your own posture. Do you sit or stand rigidly? Do you lean to one side or the other? Do you tire while standing? Could you do more exercise each day to strengthen your spine and abdominal muscles?

# Section 2 References

Many of the topics I've written about in Section 2 can be further explored in:

1. *Reflexes, Learning, and Behavior: A Window Into The Child's Mind,* Sally Goddard Blythe

2. *The Well Balanced Child: Movement and Early Learning,* Sally Goddard Blythe

3. *Disconnected Kids,* Robert Mellilo, D.C., D.A.C.N.B.

4. *Reconnected Kids,* Robert Mellilo, D.C., D.A.C.N.B.

5. *Autism,* Robert Mellilo, D.C., D.A.C.N.B.

# Section 3
# Nutrition

# Chapter 10
# A Healthy Brain Needs Three Things

*"I took a deep breath and listened to the old bray of my heart. I am. I am. I am."*

-Sylvia Plath

A healthy brain needs three things:

1. Oxygen

2. Healthy food

3. Movement

Sounds simple, doesn't it? Let's look at each of these.

**Oxygen-** Your brain needs a constant and uninterrupted supply of oxygen. Oxygen is by far the most important nutrient for your survival. Without oxygen, your cells can't make energy. Without oxygen, your brain starts to wilt. Your cells use oxygen to make a substance called ATP (adenosine triphosphate), which is the basic fuel for all brain cell activity. After just four minutes without oxygen, if you were still alive, you would very likely suffer terrible neurological consequences. No oxygen means no energy. No energy means no you.

**Healthy food-** Healthy food is important for several reasons. Your body needs a lot of good protein in order to make enzymes, hormones, cellular structures, neurotransmitters, and muscle tissue. You need a steady flow of sugar, in the form of glucose, to combine with oxygen to make ATP. You need healthy fats to build the sheathing around nerve cells, to build healthy cell walls, and to make hormones like estrogen and progesterone. You need fiber, vitamins, minerals, and water to round out a healthy diet. Your child needs all that, too, by the way.

**Movement-** Your brain is a "use it or lose it" organ. When your brain is put to use, during physical movement, conversation, study, or other activity, neurons build and maintain connections with other neurons. Activity gives the brain its consistent structure, and helps maintain a sense of where your body is in space- how to move, how fast you move, how long your muscles are, at what angle you are standing, how fast you are falling. When you stop activating your brain, by not moving, by not reading or learning new things, by not interacting with other people, your brain starts to lose synaptic connections. It becomes weak.

I hope that motivates you, on behalf of your child and yourself, to learn more about breathing, movement, nutrition, and communication.

# Questions & Action Steps

1. Can you name the three things required for brain health? Can you name them without referring back to this chapter?

2. Comment on your breath. Do you breathe deeply during the day? Do you breathe shallowly? How could you remind yourself to take deep breaths many times each day?

3. Comment on your eating habits and those of your child. Does your family consume unhealthy food? What steps could you take to improve the nutritional health of your family?

# Chapter 11
# As Much Protein As You Can Afford

*"Calories from protein affect your brain, your appetite control center, so you are more satiated and satisfied."*

-Mark E. Hyman, M.D.

Want to hear something amazing? Your body actually disassembles the protein you eat (like eggs, meat, and beans) into molecules called amino acids, and then *reassembles* them according to your physical requirements.

All proteins have value, but this varies depending on the number and quantity of different amino acids they contain. Eggs are the protein "gold standard", as they contain all essential amino acids. Animal proteins contain many essential amino acids, while plant proteins, like legumes, tofu, and grains, contain fewer.

So, exactly how much high quality protein should a person consume on a daily basis? Here's the short answer. *As much as you can afford.* In order to build the highest quality body structures, you need to have the highest quality building materials. That means the best quality protein you can afford.

The key words in the last paragraph are "high quality." Many high protein foods, especially meat, are loaded with fat, antibiotics, and artificial hormones. The best sources of protein are fresh eggs, fish, grass-fed beef (without antibiotics and preservatives), and other meat sources. In the next few years we will be hearing about a new way of getting the protein we need. The best source will remain those listed above, but packaged protein formulas called "medical foods" will become increasingly popular. These formulas are an improvement on the protein powders available at health food stores, but with a difference-- they can *guarantee* their quality and protein content. Watch for these new products. I personally think they are a breakthrough technology, and most of us will be using them in the near future.

There is a chart in your workbook illustrating the relative value of protein sources. I will cover it very carefully in the workshop. For now, I want you to remember that your body requires a lot of protein to constantly rebuild itself, and the higher quality of protein you consume, the healthier you will be.

*NOTE: There are some medical conditions that can be made worse by consuming high protein diets. Consult your physician before increasing your dietary protein, especially if you are at risk for kidney disease. The chart in your workbook gives you more information on this topic.*

# Questions & Action Steps

1. What protein sources do you eat most often? On what do you base this decision? Flavor? Cost? Availability?

2. Comment on what you've learned so far about protein. What have you learned about meat proteins? What have you learned about plant proteins?

3. Do you consume a protein powder or medical food?

4. Comment on how you budget for groceries. Do you choose foods based on quantity? Quality? Cost? Taste? Are you particular about food additives? Antibiotics? Genetic modification?

# Chapter 12
## The Problem with Sugar

*"Refined carbs raise blood sugar so quickly that the body can become immune to insulin."*

-Dr. Andrew Weil

I'm sure you've heard that our country is in the midst of a terrible obesity problem. Obesity increases your risk for heart disease and Type 2 diabetes. The consumption of refined sugar contributes greatly to this epidemic ("refined" sugar is made by removing the sugar from a plant source). Then the nutrients of the plant are discarded, leaving only the sweet tasting, but inflammation producing, sugar.

Before the advent of farming and industrialized agriculture, the only sugar we humans consumed came from plants, such as vegetables, beans, seeds, and low-hanging fruit.

In the year 1700, for instance, the average person's annual sugar consumption totaled about four pounds. Today, however, the average person consumes a whopping 160 pounds of sugar. In other words, if you ate a spoonful of sugar per day in 1700, you'd be eating 40 spoonfuls today.

We are currently over-consuming sugar to such an extent that most chronic diseases are *caused* by diet-induced inflammatory processes. The inflammatory processes are the result of high sugar consumption, insulin resistance, infections, and immune triggers like gluten.

This has a lot to do with your health and the health of your special needs child. The overconsumption of sugar and subsequent inflammatory reactions are directly linked to obesity, type 2 diabetes, Alzheimer's disease, and many other chronic degenerative disorders.

How can you know whether or not some of your child's challenges are made worse by excessive sugar consumption? Watch his or her behavior. When you limit sweets, does he or she sleep better? Communicate more clearly? Play more calmly? Move with more ease? Breathe more comfortably?

Your body requires sugar for energy production. We can't function without it. Your body uses sugar in a form called glucose. Other forms of sugar have to be converted to glucose for energy use. Glucose and oxygen enable your cells to make ATP. Your cells use ATP to make proteins.

This process works well, most of the time, *unless you consume too much sugar.* When you consume too much sugar, you store the excess energy as fat. This leads to obesity. Obesity often leads to type 2 diabetes which studies show can lead to Alzheimer's disease, heart disease, high blood pressure, stroke, and several forms of cancer.

Keep this in mind as you choose your family's meals. Long-term overconsumption of sugar is unhealthy for you and your special needs child.

# Questions & Action Steps

1. Read a few food labels at home and make a list of the sugar you consume. Include candy, ice cream, cereal, bread, pastries, pasta, potatoes, crackers, dips, soda, and fruit juice. Consider your current choices and write down your thoughts.

2. Discuss with your family how much sugar your family consumes. Can you reduce your sugar consumption and increase your consumption of fresh vegetables, beans, fish, and lean meats?

3. How could you creatively replace some of the sweets you and your child eat with healthier foods?

4. How could you encourage your child's school to serve healthy, low-sugar foods?

# Chapter 13
# Chronic Inflammation and Your Child's Brain

*"Research links chronic inflammation to a host of serious health complications, including diabetes and coronary heart disease."*

-www.livestrong.org

Along with the media buzz about sugar consumption, another health topic is beginning to gain recognition: *inflammation*. Inflammation is of key importance to you and your special needs child.

Normally, inflammation is a protective response that fights infection and rebuilds post-injury tissue. This is called "acute inflammation", and you'll notice it when, for instance, you scrape your knee. The tissue swells slightly, reddens and/or bleeds, warms, oozes a bit of pus, forms a scab, and eventually heals. In addition, white blood cells are sent to the area to thwart the spread of infection.

But *acute* inflammation is different from *chronic* inflammation. Acute inflammation is lifesaving. Chronic inflammation is actually life-*damaging*, causing terrible degenerative diseases like type 2 diabetes, Alzheimer's disease, heart disease, stroke, irritable bowel syndrome, and sleep disorders. While acute inflammation has a beginning, middle, and end, chronic inflammation goes on and on, unless you take action to stop it.

The digestive system is particularly vulnerable to chronic inflammation. Chronic intestinal inflammation is typically caused by excess sugar, red meat, grains, or antibiotic use. For example, many people have problems digesting a protein in wheat called gluten. For them, gluten is an intestinal irritant that may lead to "leaky gut" syndrome. When the intestines "leak", protein breaches the gut's protective layer and causes an inflammatory response. If this were a short-term problem, it wouldn't be serious. But for those whom gluten is an irritant, this inflammatory response is triggered every time they eat wheat-containing products, like bread. There are many other sources of intestinal inflammation, including carbonated beverages, excess coffee, many medications, and stress. Gas, bloating, and cramping are serious problems for many people, and for many children with special needs.

Even worse, the activation of gut-associated lymphoid tissue (GALT- the defense layer of your intestines) releases chemicals called cytokines that summon white blood cells to the area. Those same chemicals, in turn, activate immune cells within the lungs and brain. In other words, when a gluten-sensitive person has an intestinal immune response, inflammation occurs not only in the gut causing bloating, soreness, and sometimes nausea and bleeding, but also in the brain. Brain inflammation can result in a host of ills, including slowed brain activity, or "brain fog". Brain inflammation can be related to depression, anxiety, bipolar disorder, ADD/ADHD, and many movement disorders.

As a parent, it's your job to be armed with reliable information and make the healthiest choices possible for yourself and your child. One good choice is to provide foods and drinks that minimize chronic inflammatory responses. If your family consumes foods that provoke inflammation, like excess sugar, red meat, and gluten, it's not too late to change and heal.

# Questions & Action Steps

1. Do you notice behavioral changes when you or your child consume breads, sweets, dairy, or pasta? Do you sleep better when you avoid them?

2. Does your family have a history of type 2 diabetes, depression, Alzheimer's disease, or heart disease? Do you know what kind of diet they followed?

# Chapter 14
# Healthy Belly, Healthy Brain

*"Once a leaky gut is present, the downstream effects can be disastrous. It literally does go 'From Leaky Gut to Leaky Brain'."*

-Dr. Aristo Vojdani

We've established that a healthy brain requires oxygen, glucose, and activation. Oxygen and glucose are combined to make ATP in our cells. Activity (movement) encourages your cells to make good proteins out of amino acids. Healthy brain development depends a great deal on brain activation caused by movement.

What's that got to do with healthy intestines?

If you or your child has an intestinal problem, such as poor diet, irritable bowel syndrome, or celiac disease, the intestines are at risk for "leaking". Intestinal contents can leak through the gut wall when the wall is injured. This causes an inflammatory response that activates the body's immune system. Part of this inflammatory process takes place in the brain-associated lymphoid tissue (BALT).

When the BALT is activated, this triggers your central nervous system's microglia cells. When these cells are triggered, they initiate an aggressive immune response in your brain. Under natural circumstances, such as infection, this response would be healthy and protective. But when it results from a chronic inflammatory condition, it is very *un*healthy. Chronic microglia activation causes a decrease in your brain's ability to function properly. Some refer to this as "brain fog". Symptoms include:

- Sluggish movement
- Poor balance
- Poor memory
- Headaches
- Sleep difficulty
- Concentration problems
- Eye strain
- Trouble sequencing movements
- Poor decision making (especially about health choices like smoking, drinking, and diet)

The symptoms of a chronic microglia cell inflammation mimic those of other degenerative brain disorders. This is because when the brain is inflamed, it degenerates.

Long-term microglia cell activation is very unhealthy. If you or your child are currently experiencing symptoms of "brain fog", you can take steps to eliminate the triggers that cause it. Here's how:

**Get a blood test.** This is the best way to tell if you or your child are experiencing chronic inflammation. Request a "complete blood panel". This will test for anemia, infection, blood sugar level, inflammation, and liver function. You can also request a test for thyroid function. Other tests you might consider that would indicate heightened inflammatory processes include homocysteine, C-reactive protein, and fibrinogen.

**Analyze your eating habits.** It can be difficult to determine which food(s) might cause a reaction, especially if you are resistant to dietary changes or if your child is a finicky eater. But focus on the effect certain foods might have on the quality of your sleep and the clarity of your thinking. Do particular foods make you feel clumsy, dizzy, awkward, fatigued, or give you headaches?

**Discuss concerns with your doctor.** If your doctor is not helpful in advising you on dietary health, consider talking to a dietician or other medical specialist.

Once you've made proactive dietary and other lifestyle choices, and taken action on them, you'll reach an unprecedented level of health.

# Questions & Action Steps

1. Explain how intestinal leaks can lead to sluggish thinking. Include a brief discussion of microglia cells and their effect on brain function.

2. After meals, do you notice that your mental and physical processes become sluggish? Does this occur after all meals? Or just some? Can you identify particular foods that might be triggers?

3. Make a list of potential obstacles you may face by changing your eating habits. How could you overcome them? Write a step-by-step plan to replace inflammation-provoking foods with inflammation-reducing foods. Inflammation reducing foods include: curry, multicolored fruits and vegetables, and others listed in the *Parenting, Movement, and Nutrition* training material.

# Chapter 15
# Good Fats and Colorful Food: Choosing an Anti-Inflammatory Diet

*"The anti-inflammatory diet is a blueprint for a lifetime of optimum nutrition. Simple changes in how you eat can help counteract chronic inflammation, a root cause of many serious diseases."*

-Dr. Andrew Weil

Healthy inflammation is a natural process that protects us from infection and promotes healing. But when it becomes chronic, as discussed in the previous chapter, it leads to a host of degenerative diseases. I listed the likely foods that increase chronic inflammation: excess gluten, sugar, red meat, and pasta. Now I want to turn your attention to foods that promote health and reduce inflammation levels. There are two sources in particular:

- Omega-3 fatty acid

- Colorful vegetables, berries, and fruits

Omega-3 fatty acid is found in many foods, but is most abundant in freshwater fish, like salmon. It can also be found in flax seed, walnuts, and sardines. These healthy fats are important to your brain cells, and to all your body's cells, in order to create healthy cell membranes. Omega-3s reduce the amount of inflammatory damage to your brain brought on by poor diet, infection, or an injury like a concussion. This helps prevent heart disease and other inflammatory degenerative diseases like Alzheimer's. I strongly urge you and your child to take a daily Omega-3 supplement. Guidelines for use are contained in your workbook.

Colorful foods contain chemicals called pigments. Consuming pigments via vegetables, berries, and fruits offers a broad range of positive health affects- as plants and herbs have been used for all of recorded human history as a healing source. Another class of beneficial chemicals found in multicolored foods is flavinoids. Flavinoids, found in foods like blueberries, raspberries, and dark green vegetables, are chemicals known to reduce inflammation. They combine with other nutritional components to improve health and reduce risk of chronic disease.

There's a wonderful new health care concept called "compressed morbidity". It suggests that you can live your entire life free of chronic diseases like diabetes, heart disease, Alzheimer's, and depression, and then, at life's end, go through a relatively brief dying process. This seems preferable to years of inflammation-induced chronic disease! You can make this choice for yourself and your special needs child simply by establishing anti-inflammatory eating habits.

It's not that complicated. Cut out most refined sugars and gluten-based products, eat less red meat, reduce your dairy intake, eat a lot of colorful vegetables and fruit, increase your fish consumption, and take an

Omega-3 supplement.

If you or your child already has an inflammatory process going on, you can refer to the video training for a list of medical foods available that will reduce chronic inflammation.

# Questions & Action Steps

1. How often do you eat fish? Could you plan twice-weekly meals of freshwater salmon?

2. Where can you purchase the freshest vegetables and berries? Does your community have a farmer's market or grocery co-op? Can you increase your family's variety of multicolored produce?

3. What do you think of the concept of "compressed morbidity"? How do you feel knowing that your food choices affect not only the quality of your life, but also the quality of your death and its effect on your special needs child?

# Chapter 16
## Exercise is Nutritious

*"Deprived of the crucial opportunities for exercising the body and the senses that prepare the brain for learning in the early years, many children are literally unfit to begin the learning process."*

- Sally Goddard Blythe

When you exercise, your breathing deepens and your heart rate and blood pressure increase. By doing so, your body directs two key nutrients to your muscles and your nerve cells- oxygen and glucose. Your body coordinates this effort in order to meet the energy demands of movement. This extra glucose doesn't come directly from the food you consume; it's released from reserves that are stored in your liver. Your liver stores sugar in the form of glycogen, and when you exercise, chemical processes occur that create a steady flow of glucose. This combines with oxygen and is used in the mitochondria of your cells to make ATP. So exercise is a source of nutritious energy. If you don't use the sugar, it may be converted to fat.

It's also important to know that complex movement drives the creation of new neural connections. As you challenge yourself with complicated movements, your DNA automatically makes just the right proteins to:

- Metabolize glucose
- Build more muscle tissue
- Create intricate connections between your brain's

nerve cells
- Build proteins that convert short-term movement lessons into long-term skills

The key word is "complicated." Simple movement doesn't drive as much protein production or generate as much learning as vigorous, complicated movement. So if you want your brain to perform challenging functions, you have to exercise.

Your *Parenting, Movement, and Nutrition* movement lessons contain complicated exercises that will form new brain connections. That's not only healthy for you, but absolutely crucial for your special needs child. Your child's developing brain must be challenged by the most complex movement he or she can tolerate. Of course, if your child has a mobility-limiting disorder such as cerebral palsy, you should seek assistance from his or her physical and/or occupational therapists.

Your child cannot form many important proteins-- those brain-building substances--without practicing complicated movement. He or she needs physical challenges, such as balance, spinning, singing, catching a ball, and handling the tools of his or her daily life, like spoons, forks, plates, and bowls.

Without complicated movements, those skills don't develop. While you consider ways to enhance your child's brain function by reducing inflammation and introducing a healthier diet, I encourage you to engage in complicated movements as well. And be sure to give your child plenty of opportunities to move. Your video training contains many suggestions for nutritious exercise.

# Questions & Action Steps

1. Describe how movement initiates your brain's protein production, and how that leads to an increase in brain connections. (You can use your workbook to help you).

2. Teach this principle to a friend. Use the diagrams in your workbook to explain how brain health requires movement to create necessary proteins.

3. Comment on your experience performing your movement lessons. Can you move with ease? Do you have good balance? Is your breathing relaxed and steady?

# Chapter 17
# How to Make Each Breath More Nutritious

*"Smile, breathe, and go slowly."*

-Thich Nhat Hanh

Deep breathing is a great way to give yourself a boost of energy. Every cell in your body needs a steady supply of oxygen to maintain its ATP production. When you don't get regular, adequate oxygen, you quickly deplete your ATP. Your body doesn't maintain oxygen reserves like it does for glucose and fat. If you are oxygen-deprived for long, your cells will weaken quickly, especially your nerve cells. This is important to note for yourself and your special needs child.

Blood-oxygen levels are typically monitored in hospitals. A 95 percent saturation level is generally considered healthy. Maintaining that level is important. In fact, a large part of your brain is designated to regulate and maintain a high level of oxygen in your blood. This part of your nervous system works well most of the time, but there's a chink in the armor.

Throughout most of history, human beings were active for nearly all of their waking day. They hunted, gathered, farmed, tended to livestock, built things, and reared children. This level of movement required deep breathing; so healthy oxygen levels were easily maintained. In today's world, we are much more sedentary, and so are our children. Sedentary living, and its subsequent lack of oxygen, can lead to serious health consequences:

- It reduces your ability to perform new, brain-challenging movement.
- It reduces your oxygen demand, resulting in fatigue.
- It limits the social aspects of your brain (activity in your frontal lobe), thus limiting your interactions with others.
- It doesn't allow for adequate food metabolization, resulting in chronic intestinal inflammation, followed by brain inflammation.

What can you do to maintain healthy blood-oxygen levels and make each breath as nutritious as possible?

- Perform complex movements. This will increase your energy demand/level, improve your brain function, and reduce inflammation.
- Eat a diet loaded with anti-inflammatory foods, and reduce your exposure to pro-inflammatory foods.
- Keep a daily journal to help you stay focused, organized, and attentive to your own goals and to those of your special needs child.
- Nurture your important relationships daily, and help your special needs child build resilience, trust, and confidence.

The *Parenting, Movement, and Nutrition* movement lessons contain breathing lessons. As you perform them, memorize the exercises so that you can perform them whenever and wherever you want. They'll help you build resilience and energy and reduce stress, anytime, anywhere. Remember to breathe, deeply and often, and to help your child do the same.

# Questions & Action Steps

1. Do you typically notice your breathing? Do you take time to take deep, intentional breaths when you are stressed?

2. Have you ever taken a yoga class that focused on skillful breathing? Do you know if your community offers such a class?

3. Teach a friend about complicated movement, deep breathing, multicolored foods, and low sugar foods. Explain how these practices support your health and that of your child.

4. Describe how you'll overcome obstacles to implement healthy eating, complicated movement, and regular breathing. How much time each day would it require to achieve this? What would you be willing to sacrifice to improve your own health and that of your child?

# Chapter 18
# Eating Together is Good Medicine

*"Get people back into the kitchen and combat the trend toward processed food and fast food."*

-Dr. Andrew Weil

Eating together has a long and important role in human history. Our ancestors typically ate together, sharing the food that had been hunted, gathered, farmed, or purchased. We gathered as a community to commemorate special events like successful hunts or the changing of the seasons. Food preparation was a cooperative effort.

Eating together is one of the most satisfying of all human experiences. Sharing the smells, sounds, and tastes of food with others gives us a full, rich, sensory experience. The word companion means "the one with whom I break bread".

The way we eat has changed drastically in the past fifty years. Food technology has made food preparation quick and easy. Fast food is readily available. We no longer spend as much time together preparing meals and cleaning up afterward.

Studies show that the benefits of eating together tend to center around communities that eat Mediterranean style, where the food is locally grown and simple. Often eaten communally, these meals consisted of fish, vegetables, olive oil, simple fruits, and grain. The healthy lives of many Mediterranean communities might be a model worth our consideration. Good food and good company is good medicine.

# Questions & Action Steps

1. Does your family eat together at least once a day? Do you take time to listen to one another and share daily experiences with each other?

2. How could you engage your family in the preparation of healthy meals? Would your special needs child be able to help?

# Section 3 References

Many of the topics I've written about in Section 3 are also discussed in:

1. *The Blood Sugar Solution*, Mark Hyman, M.D.

2. *Healthy Aging*, Andrew Weil, M.D.

3. *Wheat Belly*, William Davis, M.D.

*Section 4*

*Communication*

*&*

*Leadership*

# Chapter 19
# Know Your Limitations and Get the Help You Need

*"Embracing our vulnerabilities is risky but not nearly as dangerous as giving up on love and belonging and joy."*

-Brene Brown

One of the best lessons I learned while raising my daughter was vulnerability. I was naive about parenting a special needs child, and about how much help we'd need. My life was busy. My chiropractic practice was growing, and I initially, (foolishly!) thought I could continue at that pace.

Clearly, I didn't know my limitations. At the time, I could not have recognized, much less admitted, that I was handling my life poorly. I stopped exercising. I gained 65 pounds. I gave myself type 2 diabetes.

I was not only blind to my limitations, I was ignoring offers of help and advice from loved ones.

The title of this chapter came from my counselor. One of the first things he said after we met was: "Mike, you need to know your limitations and get the help you need." As I'd acquired significant health risks, those words might have saved my life.

The amount of stress inherent in raising a special

needs child becomes even more challenging if you don't eat well, exercise, and socialize. The *Parenting, Movement, and Nutrition* training will teach you about food and movement and give you tools to improve your life. Sustaining these healthy choices beyond reading this book, and attending the workshop, will take dedication, but you will find that healthy eating, satisfying exercise, and good socialization will become a necessary and wonderful part of your life.

Taking good care of yourself is the first step. Knowing your limitations and seeking needed help will empower you to become the best parent possible.

# Questions & Action Steps

1. List five ways in which you feel vulnerable. Does admitting your vulnerability make you feel weak? Humble? Grateful?

2. List all the people who've helped you with your special needs child. Choose one and write about how he or she has improved your life. Write him or her a thank you note, and then send it to them.

3. In which areas of your life do you need the most help? Nutrition? Exercise? Socialization? What steps could you take to bring the help you need into your life?

# Chapter 20
## Your Friends Want to Help You

*"Friendship is a single soul dwelling in two bodies."*

-Aristotle

Your brain is a social organ. Without social interaction, you will lose your ability to connect with others, to learn about them, and then, in turn, to learn about yourself.

Parents of special needs children may feel socially awkward with their kids in public, especially if your child's disability is clearly evident and/or not easily understood. Very few of us are immune from feeling awkward around someone we don't know how to communicate with.

Back in high school, for instance, as I gathered with friends outside the school each morning before class, a young man with cerebral palsy occasionally walked past. When he walked, his legs scissored together and his body twisted awkwardly as he attempted to remain upright. He had difficulty talking as well. His voice sounded like a horn as he struggled to communicate. The soles of his orthopedic shoes were hard, and made a "clip-clop" sound. I felt uncomfortable watching him go past, and from the teasing he received by some of my classmates, who began calling him "Clip."

Not only did I feel humiliated by my friends' behavior, but by mine as well. I never stood up for this young man. Not once. I've thought about that often in the past 20 years, especially after my daughter was born with cerebral palsy.

What could I, or the school officials, have done differently? The teachers and administrators, who regularly witnessed the taunting, certainly should have stepped in. They might've introduced us to this young man, offering us a "teachable moment" and lessening the stigma attached to his disability.

At the time, I had no idea what "Clip's" life was like, and very little empathy for how he must have felt. All I knew was that the taunting was wrong and that I was a coward for not standing up for him. But even today, with all the advancements like wheelchair ramps, public handicap access and special education classes, most people stand on the sidelines not knowing what to do.

Here's one solution that you, as the parent of a special needs child, can do…

Ask for help.

People want to help you. Asking for help is not a sign of weakness, but of strength. On behalf of your special needs child, along with your own well-being and the enlightenment of your community, **ask for help.**

# Questions & Action Steps

1. List simple tasks with which someone could help you on occasion, such as watching your child for an hour so you can sleep, unloading groceries from your car, or going to a movie with you and your child so you have help with transportation, diapering, and feeding. You might ask a friend to attend an insurance meeting with you in order to act as a witness. Think of your needs, no matter how small, and list as many as you can.

2. Plan a time with friends to discuss your child's special needs. Focus on your presentation. Talk clearly about the strength and organization it takes to get through each day, so they see what you need. Schedule to meet at a convenient time and offer a fun, social evening. (You can use the meeting checklist in your video training for help).

3. List for yourself the positive outcome your friends will receive by helping you. Will they learn about the special needs community? Will they feel good about helping you? Will they be more supportive of school and government mandates that increase universal access for people with disabilities? Would they benefit from you teaching them a *Parenting, Movement, and Nutrition* movement lesson?

# Chapter 21
## Your Child's School Wants Him or Her to Succeed

*"Congress acknowledged that society's accumulated myths and fears about disability and disease are as handicapping as are the physical limitations that flow from actual impairment."*

–William J. Brennan, Jr., Associate Justice of the Supreme Court

In 1996, when my special needs daughter, Maren, was about to enter kindergarten, I realized how unprepared I was to properly advocate for her within our area school system. The Americans With Disabilities Act, one of the most important acts of Congress in U.S. history, had been passed just a few years before, and schools were implementing the new requirements as quickly as they could.

I attended school meetings about Maren's educational plan, feeling too incompetent to contribute to the conversation. That scared me. Once Maren was outside of my watchful eye and under the supervision of the school, I was uncertain how they'd meet her needs. Fortunately, my wife Shelly was very competent at navigating the school terrain.

The first time I attended a meeting with Maren's school team, I made it clear that I wanted Maren's school experience to be socially rich, so that she was interacting and engaged whenever possible. Our schools are committed to special needs children and are required by law to deliver a high quality education. No exceptions. You can be confident in this-- your child's school wants him or her to succeed.

To help your child's school succeed, you have to know what you want for your child. *Then you have to ask for it*. If you meet resistance, you may have to step in and champion for your child's rights. Your *Parenting, Movement, and Nutrition* workbook includes examples of positive ways to advocate on your child's behalf.

You will need to clarify your thoughts and prepare to communicate what you decide is most important for your child's school experience. Once you've thoroughly evaluated how the resulting financial and human resources would be best invested, prepare to advocate with clear language.

As we build our *Parenting, Movement and Nutrition* community, we can share information among ourselves in order to reach our goals.

# Questions & Action Steps

1. List the many means of support your child requires for school. Include physical therapy, occupational therapy, computer equipment, desk equipment, tutoring, rest, diapering, social engagement, nutritional needs, and medical/medicine attention.

2. Do you have a contact person in your child's school who will help coordinate your efforts? Is he or she likely to be a long-term ally? (If you don't know, ask). Could you schedule a breakfast or lunch meeting with this person to discuss your strategy?

3. Championing your child through school, even under the best conditions, is a long haul. What can you do to ensure that your own health and relationship needs are met? List the personal priorities and support you'll need during your parenting years. Include nutrition, exercise, alone time, and social support.

# Chapter 22
# Communicating With Your Insurance Carrier

*"There are worse things in life than death. Have you ever spent an evening with an insurance salesman?"*

-Woody Allen

This is the sad truth: insurance companies are in business to make money, not to help you. Say that a few times to yourself and let it sink in.

Health insurance companies remain financially solvent because they take in more money than they spend. We expect financial coverage for necessary health care, especially after paying our premiums faithfully for years. When basic coverage is denied, it feels like a kick in the teeth.

Insurance claim denial is a huge problem for parents of special needs children. In my experience (within my own family and the families with whom I've come in contact), I have never seen an insurance company cover all the necessary costs for cerebral palsy-related physical and occupational therapy. Not once.

If you doubt this, ask your physical or occupational therapists about their experiences with insurance companies, and whether the children they care for get all the help they need.

Communicating with insurance carriers is a skill of utmost importance. You *must* be proactive. Insurance claims adjusters are not interested in being your friend. You are a customer. Your video training contains sample letters for your insurance carrier regarding the necessity of your child's care. Since every child is different, you will need to modify the letters to fit your situation.

Here are a few things your insurer needs to know:

- Your child's diagnosis, as documented by your physician, and the physician's name.
- The name, location, and qualifications of your child's health care team, including physical therapists, occupational therapists, speech therapists, and chiropractors.
- The names of the support team at your child's school, including the school psychologist, computer assistant, school nurse, school aid, and school dietician.
- The names of hospital physicians who cared for your child and their assessment of his or her condition.

If your insurer has already denied your claims and delegated your child's case to the state (a common occurrence), the rules change. We will develop a strategy for that together as our *Parenting, Movement, and Nutrition* community grows.

For now, know that you are not alone. You will learn a lot about securing your child's rights and ensuring necessary treatment. Insurers are only able to get away with denying benefits because they know that most parents can't successfully defend medical necessity.

Together, we're going to change that.

# Questions & Action Steps

1. List the following: The person from whom you purchased your insurance, a claims contact person at your insurance company, and the person at your insurance company who makes decisions about claims payment.

2. Make a list of articles you've read about your child's condition. Sort them into two groups: articles from popular magazines and websites, and articles from peer-reviewed scientific journals. Only the peer-reviewed articles will be helpful in protecting your child. Get rid of the others, except for personal enhancement.

3. Begin to include what you've learned from your *Parenting, Movement, and Nutrition* studying in your daily journal. Albert Einstein once said that if you study a subject for just 15 minutes a day, in a few years you will be one of the world's experts on the subject. Become a passionate expert on behalf of your child and your family.

# Chapter 23
# Communicating With Government Agencies

*"Don't get officious. You're not yourself when you're officious. That is the curse of a government job."*

-Marjorie "Maude" Chardin

Government agencies include Social Security, Title 19, Aid to Families with Dependent Children, Medicare, and others. You may have dealt with several of these already.

Here's the good news-- government agencies operate *strictly* by the law. You will always know where you stand when working with these agencies, because they don't exist to make a profit. They won't try to scare you, put you on defense, or exhibit obstructive behavior like the insurance industry. You may not always get what you want, but government representatives will operate within the law.

What does that mean for you and your child? It means you need to be familiar with the law. Here are a few suggestions:

**Hire an attorney.** You may not need legal services immediately, but securing an attorney familiar with your child's condition is a good idea. When you meet, inform him or her about your child's special needs, the name of your insurance company, the name of your child's school, and the names of your child's physician(s). Ensure that the attorney agrees to represent your child if needed to secure insurance benefits, government benefits, and school opportunities.

**Study the parameters of Medicaid, Medicare, and school policies.** Your video training includes a list of resources. This task might seem overwhelming, but as you improve your body and brain with good nutrition, journaling, and your movement lessons, you will increase your ability to comprehend this kind of material.

**Get to know a social worker.** Describe your child and your family's situation. Let him or her know you are studying the law, the science, and the government policies involved with special needs parenting, and that you want to work with others to make a great life for your child. Ask him or her to do the same. If he or she doesn't take an interest in your child's case, find another social worker.

**Learn the process of filing paperwork on behalf of your child and your family.** In cases where there is a dispute with a government agency, they will often require documentation before resolving the issue.

Here's another good thing about government agencies-- their laws are subject to change. If enough of us experience a similar problem, we can contact our local and federal representatives and work to improve the system.

# Questions & Action Steps

1. Work on the above suggestions. This will take time and effort, but its worth will be invaluable.

# Chapter 24
# A Good Parent Is a Good Leader

*"To know and not to do is really not to know."*

-Dr. Stephen R. Covey

You have completed some high level training. Congratulations on your commitment, however, you are not done learning. You are on "the road less traveled". This road will remind you often; "life is difficult". The tools gathered in your *Parenting, Movement, and Nutrition* training will help strengthen your body, mind, and resolve for the work ahead.

As we finish this portion of your training, let's reassess what you've achieved:

- You've improved your knowledge on parenting, nutrition, and movement.
- You have forged a new path for your child and will help others along the way.
- You've made yourself healthier, more effective, and more focused to the benefit of your child and your family. And by doing so, you've also empowered the therapists, teachers, administrators, and government employees that you regularly deal with. You are an agent of positive change.
- As friends, family, and others notice your

- proactivity, they will begin to model their lives after yours.

A good parent is a good leader. The proactive stance you've taken on behalf of yourself and your special needs child is an admirable act of leadership.

It's been an honor to write this book and these training materials for you. I promise to further build and improve the *Parenting, Movement, and Nutrition* training as a resource for you and your child.

# Section 4 References

Many of the topics I've written about in Section 4 can be further studied in:

1. *The Seven Habits of Highly Effective People*, Dr. Stephen R. Covey

2. *The Leadership Challenge*, Barry Posner & Jim Kouzes

3. *Encouraging The Heart*, Barry Posner & Jim Kouzes

4. *The Emotional Life of Your Brain*, Richard Davidson, Ph.D.

5. *The Road Less Traveled*, M. Scott Peck, M.D.